The Time Is Now!

*A Map illustrating
the War of the Oceans
appears in a center spread
of this book*

The Time Is Now!

BY PIERRE VAN PAASSEN

Author of Days of Our Years

THE DIAL PRESS

NEW YORK : 1941

COPYRIGHT, 1941
BY PIERRE VAN PAASSEN

PRINTED IN THE UNITED STATES OF AMERICA
BY THE HADDON CRAFTSMEN, INC., CAMDEN, N. J.

To the Reader

ALTHOUGH I had recently become engaged in the writing of a book of a more contemplative character, I was forced to interrupt my labors when the full dire extent of the Nazi menace to America galvanized me into action. Today I am utterly convinced that the threat to our national security and to the peaceful evolution of our democratic institutions is no longer something remote or vague, or that it can still form the subject of speculation on such eventualities coming to pass as the fall of the battered and quaking British Commonwealth. I have come to the realization that the threat which confronts us in America is direct, and that we stand in immediate and mortal danger now. For that reason, I think that if America is to continue to exist as a free and independent nation, drastic and heroic and revolutionary measures are in order now. That is to say, we must strike hard, immediately and without relenting, at the deadly and declared foe of all that we hold dear and sacred, until he is finally brought low.

My reasons for these beliefs I have set forth here briefly and without literary solicitude. At times I have used the language of the Bible, because that is the language of the American people.

Forasmuch as there may be some who will wonder that one who was a determined opponent of war should now advocate recourse to arms, I say that I still believe war a supreme evil and its existence on earth today the result of the betrayal of Christ by organized Christianity. But I do not think that spiritual defense and prayers and

5

words alone will protect us against the onrushing forces which are intent on blotting out Christianity and democracy forever. Today I feel that I must take to heart the words that were engraved on the walls of their dungeons in Nîmes by the captive but undaunted Huguenots: *"Résistez! Battez-vous!* Resist! Fight!"*

PIERRE VAN PAASSEN

New York
May 1, 1941

I

WE ARE living in an insane world. Our puritan ancestors would have called it a world possessed of the devil. But what distinguishes the era of historical transition through which we are passing from other, previous epochs wherein human society was transformed from top to bottom is the fact, pointed out by Dr. Huizinga, that we know ours to be an age of decline and of disintegration. Nobody was really surprised when peace was interrupted again in 1939 and the guns began to speak. England may have slept, as Winston Churchill had it; France may not have been prepared to withstand the onslaught of a ruthless enemy; and America may not have been interested, or pretended not to have been interested, in a matter it thought of no concern to itself: that ever-recurrent turmoil of clashing and contradictory forces and interests over there in Europe. Even so, there had been for several years and throughout the world a constantly deepening disquietude and anxiety about the future. The watchmen and the guardians of the things of the spirit—that is, the dreamers and the poets and the idealists—had sent up signal after signal of an approaching thunderstorm. So the masses of the peoples too, in the end, gained the disturbing impression that something had gone seriously wrong. From time to time we all had that sinking feeling, a feeling that our civilization was collapsing.

Now, this gloomy presentiment of disaster did not come to torment us solely in the empty hours of the night when the flame of life burns low, when courage sinks with the deepening of shadows, and the field of our observation becomes peopled with all sorts of fantastic images. No; when we sensed that grave and far-reaching events were bearing down upon us and that a new historical cataclysm might be lying around the next bend in the road, this feeling rested on sober judgment and on observation. The facts stared us in the face. And they still do, for that matter.

Today we see that the pillars of society have begun to tremble, that the foundations of truth and humanity, reason and justice, which we thought enduring and of permanent value, have begun to disintegrate. "There are social systems which no longer function and economic systems that are lying on their deathbeds." It is a condition for the creation of a new humanity that the world become penetrated by a conception of the essential dignity of the human personality and, in a larger sense, of the need and the right of nations to coöperate freely—each to contribute according to its own character, in a personal-national sense—towards the sum total of civilization in the construction of the new earth. This condition is in danger of being swept away by a new philosophy which some would identify as the "wave of the future," but which could more truly be denounced as the return of the age of tyranny.

What we witness in our time is a growing desolation of the things of the spirit and the rise of a dictatorship of Mammon and Moloch, those idols of antiquity whom the Hebrew people encountered when they entered the Promised Land. In our time, these idols have taken on the shape and form of a quasi-almighty super-state, a state which depersonalizes the individual, which dehumanizes man and will ultimately bestialize him if no resistance is offered. Even now it is turning man into

8

a mere automaton, an article to be bartered in the market place.

Of course, there have been men, philosophers and sociologists, who for a long, long time have been warning us that all was not well with our world. For years these men, in their rôle as awakeners of man's conscience, have pointed to the exact spot and the precise hour where history went wrong—or, rather, where man turned up the wrong way. Long before the industrial system had reached its zenith there were men who warned that it had been built up, as Bishop Gore once said, "in a profound revolt against the central law of Christian morality: Thou shalt love thy neighbor as thyself." There are, in fact, few things in history more astonishing than the silent acquiescence of the Christian world in the radical betrayal of its ethical foundation.

But we paid no heed to the prophets of the modern day, any more than the Jews in ancient times heard those that spake to the fathers in divers manners and in many places. We simply do not like to listen to what we call the voice of pessimism. All our life, our public life especially, is geared to the spirit of blithe optimism. We would rather drift blindly and aimlessly, with some fitful slogan on our lips about "prosperity being right around the corner," than take a realistic account of our environment and of the road we are traveling.

Yet today the "pressing uneasiness" that weighed upon the minds of but a few has become well-nigh general, if not universal. The consciousness that we are passing through a very grave crisis of civilization is permeating every layer of society in every land under the sun. We are fast becoming habituated to the thought —difficult though it is to accept it—that things we at one time considered to be self-evident, such as human progress, are not so sure at all. Our civilization may pass, as

9

other civilizations have passed and are now catalogued in the department of forgotten things. The very word "progress" scarcely appears in the spoken and written vocabulary of our time.

What numbs our hearts with fear and with apprehension is no longer an evil nightmare that vanishes with the first crack of dawn and the first chirp of the birds. In our waking hours we see the spectacle of black night descending upon the world, of one nation after the other passing under the yoke of the new slavery, and of the great majority of the human race threatened with reduction to the rank of coolies. In dread anticipation of more evil tidings we turn our eyes away from newspapers, and nervously switch the dial on our radios to escape hearing the harbingers of fresh disasters. One day we are swept on to the highest pinnacle of hope and faith in the future, only to be pushed back on the morrow, like the mercury in a thermometer, into the pit of somber despair. Where are the prophets now who warned us in the past that this would come? The cry goes up for guides to make us see the road ahead. Should we, as Americans, draw back in our shell, fearful of the foe? Or should we step forward resolutely into the arena, as did our ancestors, who quailed before no danger?

We debate those questions and rack our brains until we grow weary and doubly uncertain. Paralysis creeps in, and fear begins to deaden our senses. We begin to look for an outlet for pent-up emotions, for a scapegoat on whom to unload our mistrust and secret fears. We are growing suspicious of one another, and are becoming inclined to listen to the voice of the beguiler, as the people of France did before us: "Is Labor really playing the game?" "Can the Jews be trusted?" "Is not our educational system at fault?" One day we censure the Government for not leading the way, and the next we protest that we are being pushed too rapidly. We have even begun to distrust democracy as the true way of life, and more and more of us are inclined to bow our heads as in resignation to our fate.

Wist ye then not that these things must be? You say that it is a pity, an injustice that the innocent should have to suffer with the unrighteous; that nations, therefore, as well as individuals who did not seek war should not be called upon to share its horrors.

Where are the innocent? Who chased the great apostle of the League of Nations, Woodrow Wilson, into the blackness of the night? Who ridiculed that first attempt to establish an international order sanctioned by international justice and agreement, and called it unrealistic and Utopian and the folly of dreamers and professors? Who withdrew from Europe after making the world "safe for democracy," instead of keeping it safe? Were not "normalcy" and prosperity considered more imperative than seeing to it that the old hearths of rancor and hatred should not flare up again? What was the response of President Roosevelt's suggestion, three long years ago, that the aggressor nations should be quarantined?

There are no innocents. The guilt of the innocent resides in the fact that it is they who gave power to the evil-doers. It is through our own cowardice and lukewarmness to the ideals of democracy that the forces of evil have gained the enormous power they wield in the world at present. Fundamentally, it is a case of the so-called innocent having made the evil-doers what they are today.

The peculiarity of present-day forms of evil is not the enormity of the evil but the enormity of its power. For who are these men: Hitler, Mussolini and Stalin? Are they extraordinarily important men, or particularly gifted men? In a moral sense they are not more important than others; intellectually they are scarcely above the average. But they are filled with egoism. They are bereft of all sense of responsibility toward God, which means that they are not orientated toward their fellow human beings as brothers. In that respect they are very much like ourselves. But they have been given power—power such as no human soul can support, power without limit, over life and death. This has led them to feel that they owe responsibility to no one, neither to God nor man. "The Duce is always right." "The Fuehrer stands between God and the German nation." "Stalin is the father of the peoples, the greatest shepherd and leader of all time." The suggestion that these men are divine or semi-divine is made even now.

The question is asked: How did evil get on the throne in the first place?

Where were the good and the innocent, those who knew the difference between good and evil, between the lie and the truth, when evil first raised its head in the form in which it menaces us today? Did they speak out? Did they raise their voices? Did they resist the emerging power of evil or brand it with their searing word? Where were the representatives of decency, of justice, intelligence and religion, when Hitler proclaimed his Aryan myth and proceeded to disenfranchise and then torture the Jews? Were they heard from? Or were we told instead that it was no concern of ours what went on in Germany? And in that hour when the marauders proceeded to close the schools, burn books, crush the labor organizations and turn great old universities into drill halls, what did the world hear from the scholars and men of learning, the free men of the spirit as a collective body? A few pleaded for tolerance and expressed their indignation—but only a very few. They were the exceptions, and they soon drew condemnation on themselves as meddlers unworthy of the traditions of scholarly dignity and decorum.

Would Erasmus have been silent, or would Castellio and Spinoza and Fray Luis de Leon and Voltaire and Edgar Quinet have held their peace? Or is it true, as John Viénot once remarked sarcastically, that if the men of the spirit once began to concern themselves with the demands of justice, they would no longer be men of the spirit?

The root of the present-day evil resides not only as a Frenchman has said, in *la trahison des clercs*—the betrayal of the intellectuals—but in the abdication of the decent.

"Did you ever hear the story," Leonard Ragaz, the great Swiss reformer once asked me, "of that priest in the Alcazar fortress of Toledo who came to the commandant in the course of the siege with a suggestion of surrender or, failing that, of at least sending the women and children away to safety? The commandant angrily turned the priest away with the words: 'Man, don't bother me. Give us all absolution, and we will all die together.'

"Well," went on Dr. Ragaz, "if democracy is not able to inspire its followers with the same heroism as those Spaniards displayed, then its cause will not only be lost in our time—then it is lost now!"

I still do not believe that armaments and still more armaments were the safeguards of democracy. The basis of enduring peace is an international order based on justice and respect for minorities. The first feeble attempt to establish such an order, however, we ourselves helped sabotage, by calling it unrealistic and by laughing at the dreamers of human brotherhood and of the world's federation.

The forces of evil rampant in the world today found

a place that was already prepared for them. The ground was cleared for their emergence into the light of day because of our own lack of vigilance, because we paid only lip-service to democracy and regarded it merely as the comfortable *status quo* in which our nation and our class enjoyed a measure of well-being.

Theology, too, took all possible pains to furnish the so-called Militia Christi—the Christian soldiers who should be marching onward, but who are and for years have been retreating as fast as they can—with a clean sheet and a clear conscience before the arrival of the forces of paganism and brutality. "Give Caesar what is Caesar's and God what is God's," was the prescription. Factually it meant that life in its entirety was abandoned to unscrupulous and ruthless force. For God there remained a small, still corner in the church; but the preaching of the gospel of freedom for all was eviscerated of every matter of vital importance to the people.

As a boy I once visited some relatives in Limburg, one of the southeastern provinces of Holland. Not far from the town, across the Belgian border, lay a district known as Moresnet, which on pre-war maps was designated as neutral territory. It belonged neither to Belgium, Holland nor Germany. Gypsy tribes roamed the place, but no police of any sort were ever seen there. It was, indeed, a most romantic and strange region. One day, during one of our walks, we encountered an old man in the woods of Moresnet; in a mysterious voice he told us that deep, deep in the forest lay an abandoned mine and that gold could still be extracted from it, if one would do the necessary digging. Driven by love of adventure and the thirst for gold, we found the mine at last. But in order to go down into the shaft where the old man said the treasure lay, we would have had to venture onto a decrepit and water-soaked old ladder which pointed down into that dark but tempting deep. We debated a long time, but no one of us had the courage to descend into the shaft. In the end we were greatly relieved when one of our companions discovered that the stones lying about the mouth of the shaft contained gold. We were overjoyed, and believed ourselves as rich as the Burgomaster of Amsterdam. We gathered the rocks and loaded them into sacks, dragged them all the way home—only to learn that we had been fooled. What we had taken for the precious metal was fool's gold, or *klatergoud*, as the Dutch say.

I fear that many of us grown-up children today have had a similar experience. We have mistaken the glittering, easily accessible fool's gold lying on the surface, for the real thing that lies hidden in the depths, that can be extracted only by patience and courage, and with adequate tools. Today is the hour of disillusionment and disenchantment.

But not only of disenchantment. Today should also be the time of repentance, of acknowledgment of guilt, of contrition and of penance. We have, in the words of the prayerbook, done those things which we ought not to have done and left undone those things which we ought to have done. If that repentance is to be sincere, we must recognize and acknowledge that we, too, have had our share in the production of the catastrophes which have come over the world. We must confess that whereas once, after the last war, we were offered a new goal in life and a new right, we neglected to take advantage of our opportunities. Instead, we washed our hands of Europe; we failed to protect the new freedom by our great moral authority, and subsequently we looked on with smugness and vainglorious pride, undisturbed and insensitive, while freedom and justice and decency were trodden underfoot in one place after the other.

With the repentance there must come a moral regeneration, a reawakening of fraternal responsibility for the weary and heavy-laden in our own land and for men of good will everywhere.

Such an act of national rededication would, indeed, be the return to democracy and to God. For then also would we, as a nation, find forgiveness, and by God's good grace be given a new strength, a new chance, a new goal in life and a new right to live.

What stands before the door is the supreme test of whether our repentance has been sincere, whether we shall be judged worthy to go forward as a free nation.

II

WHEN, after every blow Hitler deals out, political commentators and interpreters use their pet phrase about the Fuehrer's next move being anybody's guess, they may very well be in earnest, in so far as the extent of their own perception is concerned. But they thus foster, albeit unconsciously, that spirit of irresolution—the planlessness and the paralyzing inactivity on the part of the democracies—which has been the surest guarantee of Hitler's success so far. For if we do not know where the next blow is going to fall, how can we hope to parry it? If we are left in the dark as to Germany's fundamental plan of strategy for the conquest of the world, how will we know whether one of Hitler's moves on the international chessboard, which at first sight may seem to be of but secondary importance, does not in reality constitute the master stroke of history, in that it seals the fate of our own country?

To many observers, amongst them a number of statesmen, the civil war in Spain at one time appeared to be nothing more significant than a bloody dispute between adherents of two equally obnoxious ideologies, Fascism and Communism. Whichever of the two contending parties came out victorious seemed, therefore, a matter of supreme indifference. Only in 1941 did it become clear that Franco's early victories in 1937 had laid the ground for Hitler's final blow to Great Britain's Mediterranean position in 1941.

The comment on the uncertainty of Hitler's next moves is as absurd as if a baseball writer were to question whether a player standing on third base would make a dash for home plate on the first base-hit. Hitler is by no means running around in aimless circles, even though it may at times appear that he is on a senseless rampage. The German General Staff is not on a wild goose chase, darting to and fro to snatch plums from the trees the moment the policeman's back is turned.

The Nazis are operating according to plan. They have time and again revealed the existence of that plan and have even publicized its most minute details. It is true that their plan is so fantastic that few people outside of Germany ever took it seriously. The details of this immense project are, moreover, scattered in thousands of books and pamphlets and wrapped up in such obtuse and technical language that the underlying thought can be disentangled only with a more than Job-like patience by the non-military, non-oceanographic and non-geopolitical layman.

The present hostilities, which got under way in 1938 with the destruction of that great military bastion that was the Czechoslovak Republic and with the crushing of Spanish democracy, show day by day that the Germans are following their plan to the letter. They are taking the world by installments. Yet none of Hitler's successive *blitzkrieg* invasions must be looked upon as the main battle. His conquests in Central Europe, of the Scandinavian and Low Countries, of the Balkans and the Near East are but stages in a campaign that will not stop until every knee in the entire world is bent in humble subjection. Prague, Oslo, Amsterdam, Paris, Belgrade, Cairo, Teheran, Cape Town, Calcutta, Rio de Janeiro and Valparaiso are but milestones on the road to the final goal. Hitler is forging the links of a chain which, if finally connected, will place the entire human race under a yoke—a yoke which, so the German strategists plan, will not be shaken off for a thousand years to come.

The sooner the leaders and the peoples of the few remaining free countries understand the gigantic scope and pattern of the present hostilities, the more chance there will be of stopping Hitler. The more time they spend in idle speculation about Hitler's next moves and in reassuring one another that British diplomacy and British staff work are outwitting the Fuehrer at every turn—disrupting his spring schedule today, and forcing him to fight in an area he had not chosen or foreseen tomorrow—the sooner the steel net which Germany is weaving around the world, including the United States, will be closed. Then, indeed, will all further thought of resistance become futile and hopeless.

The first principle we must recognize is that the Nazi army is on the march to defeat the British navy. This is the war of the oceans, and Hitler is winning that war without a navy.

The war of the oceans is the plan of the Geopolitical Institute of Germany, the Reich's political and military planning academy. Let us pause here for a moment to trace the development of the Geopolitical Institute. It will perhaps help us to understand contemporary events.

The Geopolitical Institute was discovered by America —in 1939! Actually it has existed since 1897, and its ideology has fermented in the minds of German political thinkers since 1870. It is significant that we were more than four decades late in recognizing the fact that the German government—whether a *Kaiserreich*, republic or totalitarian state—enthusiastically sponsored a planning academy whose function was to develop a long-range project for the domination of the

19

world. Even today when I mention that the Geopolitical Institute at Munich is a huge collective brain center that guides Herr Hitler's every step, I am met with skeptical smiles or I am denounced as a war-monger propagandizing for the British government. Yet to deny that the Geopolitical Institute has for almost half a century been evolving a scheme to conquer the world would be to falsify history.

Geopolitical thinkers were not happy during Bismarck's régime. The Iron Chancellor did not believe either in colonial expansion or in Germany's future on the seas. As a matter of fact, it was his rather brusque veto of the young Kaiser Wilhelm's imperialistic schemes that brought about Bismarck's fall. In those days, fifty years ago, political observers were mystified by the abrupt split between Europe's dean of statesmen and young Wilhelm the Second. Officially, the issues leading to the dropping of the pilot of Germany's foreign policy dealt with the prolongation of the anti-Socialist law and other far-reaching labor legislation. But the real conflict was based on Kaiser Wilhelm's adoption of geopolitical ideas then sponsored by the Institute of Political Oceanography (which later was taken over by the Geopolitical Institute). Kaiser Wilhelm believed in Germany's destiny as mistress of not only Europe but of the whole world.

Friedrich Ratzel, who died in 1904 and who is today glorified by geopoliticians as the pioneer of the oceanographic movement, is credited with influencing Kaiser Wilhelm in his naval ambitions. Ratzel's formula, when stripped of its ponderous and involved phraseology, can be expressed as follows:

"The world is seventy-two per cent water and twenty-eight per cent land. Any power that aims to dominate the world must control its waterways. The oceans—

not the land—influence historical changes. At no time has a single power dominated all the known areas of the world. But there have been historical eras when only a single war fleet exercised complete sovereignty over the oceans, and thus controlled the world—the Roman fleet after the destruction of Carthage, for example, and the English navy after the fall of Napoleon. If the Germans are to fulfill their destiny and become the masters of the world, they must reinforce their invincible army with just as powerful a fleet. This means that they must either make Britain their ally and partner or, if that should prove impossible, compel the British to surrender their fleet and shipbuilding wharves. Nothing can prevent the Germans from accomplishing this task except a failure to recognize that the capture of the road to world conquest leads over the waterways."

That is the fundamental maxim of Germany's geopolitical planners. At present the waterways are policed by the British navy. In order to wrest that control out of Britain's hands, Germany must defeat the British navy. It would therefore have seemed logical, at first glance, for Germany to have poured all her energy and wealth in the creation of a fleet powerful enough to challenge the British. That is, in fact, what the Kaiser did. He built so strong a navy that his uncle of England, King Edward VII, warned him that Britain would not countenance so mighty a rival in the Atlantic. Wilhelm, it is said, tried to reassure his uncle that the German navy was intended for use against the United States, not against England. But British naval authorities were far from reassured.

It is well known that, a few years before the first World War, Admiral Jack Fisher, after viewing a visiting squadron of the German fleet at anchor in the

Thames, sought an audience with King Edward and said to him: "Your Majesty, the Germans are enlarging their canal linking the Baltic with the North Sea. They are also increasing their first-class navy. As soon as they are ready, they will seek war with Britain on some pretext or other. I think that just as a precaution we ought to sail into the Baltic forthwith and sink the German fleet without warning and without a declaration of war. If we don't, we will rue our inactivity some day!"

When the test came, however, the Kaiser's navy proved no match for British power. The English turned the tables on Wilhelm, and with their allies launched armies that marched overland and forced the German navy to surrender.

Hitler—or, rather, the geopoliticians—did not fail to learn from the mistakes of the Kaiser. The Nazis did not build a new fleet to take the place of the ships which went down to the bottom of Scapa Flow in 1919.

A study of Hitler's foreign policy up to the Spanish "civil" war gives evidence that the Geopolitical Institute wavered between a pro-English policy, leading to a partnership, and a pro-French policy aiming to isolate England. This indecision was due to the difficulty the Institute, under General Haushofer, was experiencing in evolving a program to overcome the weakness of the German navy. But when Hitler's planning body presented him with the new tactics he no longer courted British favor.

What is this new plan that Hitler is now so skilfully executing?

It is the "march around the oceans." Hitler's armies are driving to those shores from which the shipping lanes of the world can be dominated. In the present battle the German army is being pitted against the British navy. And the way things have been going this year, it appears that Herr Hitler will win the Battle of the Pacific, as well as the Battle of the Atlantic, without invading the British Isles. For he is making a mockery of navies and upsetting all previously conceived theories of sea warfare.

The American people's eyes are riveted on the Atlantic, and they are made to see nothing worse than the sinking of British ships, whose faster or slower disappearance serves as a sort of barometer by which they gauge the stability of British staying power on the beleaguered island. Hitler, meanwhile, proceeds to surround the waters of the earth's surface and to drive British ships from their harbors and bases.

Of what use will navies be, if they have nowhere to land, nowhere to take on ammunition, nowhere to go for repairs? They will become useless, and will be forced either to sail into the enemy's hands to be surrendered, or be scuttled at sea.

The war of the oceans is no idle boast. Gradually, as the smoke and dust lift over the battle fields, the geographic significance of Hitler's conquests reveals itself: the Nazi military moves conform strictly to the design mapped out by the Geopolitical Institute, and the goal is the domination of the oceans.

Look at the map—or, rather, at the globe, as Walter Lippmann, who is versed in geopolitical science, has been urging the American people to do these many months. Many of us seem to forget these days that the world is round and that there is a very real interrelationship between the oceans.

Now what can we observe about the huge expanses of water that cover nearly three quarters of the globe's surface?

Examining first the Mediterranean, we see that it is the smallest of the seas and that through Suez and the

Red Sea it connects the Atlantic with the Pacific. The Mediterranean is the center of the hub from which the world's seaways radiate in all the directions of the compass. But even as it links the Atlantic and the Pacific, so it can also be made to separate these two oceans. Great Britain has hitherto safeguarded the uninterrupted connection because of the geographical dispersion of her possessions and dominions in the two oceans. She has maintained the safety of the route to her Far Eastern empire by establishing naval bases, and in later years air bases, on the shores and in the proximity of the navigation channels of the Mediterranean—at Gibraltar, on Malta, on Crete and Cyprus, in Palestine and Egypt.

The first step Germany had to take, therefore, in her attempt to gain control of the Eastern hemisphere, was to break the link connecting the various parts of the British, French and Dutch empires, by attacking the Mediterranean. Long ago the Geopolitical Institute prescribed the following preparatory moves for the conquest of the Mediterranean basin:

1. An Alliance with Italy.
2. Control of the coasts of Spain.
3. Control of Albania.
4. Control over France.
5. Control over Spanish Morocco, French Morocco, Algiers and Tunis.
6. Control over Libya and Egypt.
7. The establishment of at least two continuous overland routes from Germany to the shores of the Old World's sea; for instance, through France and Spain, through Jugoslavia and Greece or through Turkey and Palestine.

Once these points are established, there follows the

mere formality of closing the two exits at Suez and Gibraltar. I call it a formality because, with virtually the entire coast line of the Mediterranean in Germany's hands or in the hands of Germany's partners—Italy, Spain and France—the British navy will be rendered impotent. Indeed, whatever British naval units happen to be in any part of the Mediterranean when Germany locks the exits will be trapped, or will have to fight their way out under particularly perilous circumstances.

Such is the German strategy for the Battle of the Mediterranean. Planned to its smallest detail, it began with the Spanish civil war. The second great war of the twentieth century actually broke out in July, 1936, following the experience in defying the League of Nations and developing a technique of camouflaged war which had been gained by Japan in Manchuria and Italy in Abyssinia. The direct assistance which Italy gave with aircraft and the indirect assistance which Germany gave with warships (to transport Franco's troops from Africa to Spain) were the first operations of the present war: they were Hitler's first moves to destroy the British Empire.

What followed in the Mediterranean theatre, in the Far East, in Scandinavia, in Central Europe and the Balkans, was equivalent to maneuvering for position before delivering the main blow.

On March 15, 1938, the British General Staff sent a "note of elucidation" to the Secretary of State for War in which occurred the following observation of the utmost gravity:

"People who talk of preventing another great war are already twenty months out of date. . . . We in this country [England] have failed to see that the war is now in progress. . . . [This] is due to the fact that we are still thinking politically, whereas the dictatorship states are thinking militarily. . . .

"The situation in this new great war as it stands now [March, 1938] would seem to be that the enemy is within reach of gaining the decisive points without a battle, and in the most vital direction we have made no serious attempt to prevent him.

"Armament programs merely belong to the grand tactics of this modern kind of war. They are vain if you are beaten strategically. We have been courting this risk."

That risk had become a tragic reality in May, 1941!

Germany's long-range preparations prove that the war of the oceans is not meant to be a *blitzkrieg*. Only the battles necessary to acquire the land bases are planned as short, quick knock-out blows. That this is so can readily be gauged from the long interval that elapsed between Franco's entry into Madrid and the German army's march into Poland, between the Polish victory and the invasion of the Low Countries, and, once more, between the collapse of France and the attack on Jugoslavia. Altogether more than two years.

They were years of patient diplomatic scheming, of a war of nerves, of painstaking preparations and, finally, of well-timed military blows when these could no longer be avoided. This game of waiting and political blackmail carefully follows the geopolitical recipe, which counsels armed conflicts only as a last resort. Hitler himself expressed this policy in a recent speech when he said: "Who would be so mad as to take by force anything that he could get by reason?"

As Spain led to Czechoslovakia and Czechoslovakia to Poland, and as France led to the Balkans and to the conquest of the Mediterranean, so the Mediterranean does not constitute the final objective in Hitler's plans.

All that occurred up to the virtual closing of the Mediterranean to British shipping was but a preliminary to the real campaign to come. As Holland was taken not for its own sake but rather to serve as a stepping-stone to new conquests, and Jugoslavia was invaded not merely to revenge an affront to the Fuehrer but to become a jumping-off place for an attack, diplomatic or military, on Turkey and Egypt, so the conquest of the Mediterranean is not an end in itself, but rather the beginning of the Battle of the Oceans.

Just as the oceans intermingle and flow into one another, so also Germany's plans for the war of the oceans interlock at certain periods and frequently are in simultaneous progress. While the Mediterranean battle is still unfolding, the Pacific and Atlantic battles have already begun. It is, however, quite obvious that the Pacific battle cannot enter its final stage before the Battle of the Mediterranean is successfully concluded. Nor can the Battle of the Atlantic proceed much further until Gibraltar is under German control.

Geopolitical views—and we must reckon with them— are extremely flexible concerning the sequence of the battles of the Pacific and the Atlantic. They are guided by the measure of political and military resistance. Thus, any political weakness on the part of Washington in the Pacific would immediately accelerate the strategic plans in that ocean. On the other hand, any sign of a decline of morale on the British Isles would undoubtedly bring about a supreme effort on Hitler's part to administer the *coup de grace* in the Atlantic first. But whether the war of the oceans, after the Mediterranean interlude, proceeds full force to the Pacific or to the Atlantic is relatively unimportant. The fate of the United States is at stake in either event.

"War is an art. A great warrior must be a sensitive

27

musician. He must be able to combine the most contrasting tones, chords and rapidly changing tempi, and fuse them into one great whole." These words are credited to Adolf Hitler during an intermission at a Wagnerian festival, and are often referred to by the German press. They are used to illustrate Hitler's versatility in employing simultaneously every possible political and military source of strength in the present conflict. Like the conductor of a symphony, so say his admirers, he indicates when and where the emphasis should be placed. Today a *fortissimo* air attack on England, tomorrow an *allegro con forza* submarine onslaught in the Atlantic, next week a *staccato* ultimatum to Pétain, and the next day a new *arpeggio* to arouse harmonic overtones in Spain, while at the same time the Tokyo trumpets are made to blare stridently in the direction of the United States to add a new fuel to political disunion in our country.

Hitler, the artist-warrior, is of course conducting in accordance with the score placed before him by the Geopolitical Institute. In this score the Pacific intermezzo is covered by the following series of steps, some of which will be recognized as already having been inaugurated or completed.

1. A Soviet-Japanese pact. This Hitler had pledged to Tokyo quite some time ago because Nippon refused to coöperate with Berlin unless the Soviet peril were removed from its back door.
2. Political control, including aërial and submarine bases along the Hejaz-Asir-Yemen coast line down to Aden.
3. Control of Iraq, the Mosul oil fields, Persia and Afghanistan. Strategically this move no longer belongs to the Battle of the Mediter-

ranean, but is a vital part of the Pacific phase. It is designed not only for the replenishment of Germany's oil supply, but also to provide possible bargaining areas for the New World Order in its discussions with the Soviets and Turkey—and, of course, to fulfill the old dream of the Berlin-Bagdad line.

4. Control over India—primarily economic, and divided with the Soviets.

5. Control over Siam and Indo-China, through the Asiatic Axis partner.

6. Seizure, by Japan, of Singapore, the Dutch East Indies, Borneo and the Philippines, cutting off England from the Pacific except via the long Panama route.

7. Simultaneous consolidation of control over the entire African continent, a comparatively easy undertaking because of French colonial impotence, insufficient British military strength in the Anglo-Egyptian Sudan, Ethiopia and Kenya, and the strong anti-British sentiment among the Boers in South Africa.

This truly epic campaign, which borders on the incredible, is clearly projected by the German planners today. They schedule it not for some distant future, but actually as the follow-up of the Mediterranean battle. Unless we completely rid ourselves of the horse-and-buggy idea that the present struggle is just another European war, we cannot grasp the vast scope of these Nazi schemes. This is a game in which the chips are no mere countries, but continents. It is a gamble in which all the cards have been reshuffled and all the rules suspended. Hitler is playing to break the Anglo-Saxon bank—or, as he calls it, "the British-American plutocracy's hegemony over the world." But military experts will have to agree that this program can be executed no matter what the British navy may do to prevent it.

The African chapter, even apart from its strategic significance in the war of the oceans, is regarded by the Geopolitical Institute as the most important. For the entire African continent has been earmarked as a German colony to supply the necessary raw materials to the industrial plants working for the Nazi overlords in the New Europe. Historically and geopolitically Africa belongs to Germany, say Hitler's planners of the New Order.

"When this war is over," writes Ignaz Appel, one of the chiefs of the Geopolitical African Department, "a new era will begin for Africa too. Hitherto England and France have managed Africa in the manner of a business corporation run for the benefit of only a few shareholders. Tomorrow the administration of this continent will be a German task. Because of their pioneer work, the Germans are entitled to undertake this great task of colonization. Heretofore the Mediterranean has played the false rôle of a dividing sea. From now on it will, geographically and politically, play the rôle of a connecting inland lake. The reorganization of Africa by the vigorous forces of the New Europe [the Nazi-controlled Europe] is politically and economically essential. The New Europe will, for the first time in history, see to it that Africa's wealth of raw materials will bring to our nation a constant rise in its standard of living."

In the Battle of the Pacific the African conquest assumes extraordinary importance, because its strategic significance spills over into the Battle of the Atlantic. Nazi domination over Africa *ipso facto* places the entire eastern shore of the Atlantic, from Cape Town to Trundheim (with the exception of the English isle) under the aërial and submarine control of Hitler's war-machine. Besides, it paves the way for a final contest with the United States for preponderant influence over South America. The distance from Dakar to Natal, for instance, is less than half that from New York to the Brazilian port. And what an excellent take-off point Africa represents for a close political *rapprochement* with South America! All the signs indicate a strong-hand "good neighbor policy" between Hitler and the South American republics. But whatever type of political pressure Hitler uses against the United States via South America, one incontrovertible fact will then be understood even by those who answer all arguments about the Nazi danger to America with that phrase about three thousand miles of Atlantic Ocean: that fact is that the "wave of the future," with Hitler riding it, will be beating violently against the Western hemisphere. The war of the oceans will be right at our own front door.

"South America is waiting for us," cries the German press. The Western hemisphere, just like the Old World, has its own Mediterranean problem, the Nazis claim. The Central American republics on the shores of the "American Mediterranean Sea"—that is, the Caribbean—also are dominated by a great power, just as Italy, in the past, has been dominated by England. They too find the gateway to the ocean artificially closed to them: to wit, the Pacific Ocean, by the American-controlled Panama Canal. It is by means of the Panama Canal, Germany charges, that Washington intends to relegate Latin America to a colonial status. But, warn the Germans, the Latin Americans are fully aware of their own strength and of ours, and "Roosevelt's plan to enslave Central and South America" will—nay, *must*—be brought to naught.

As for the famous Battle of the Atlantic which alone,

according to some experts, is going to decide this conflict—it may never be fought, just as the Maginot Line of France never was attacked. The aërial onslaughts on England, even if they cannot break Britain's spirit, are gradually reducing her armament production to a negligible quantity, while the German submarine guerrilla warfare is depended upon to transform the Atlantic water routes to England into cemeteries for American aid to Britain. "We are using less than ten thousand men in the Battle of the Atlantic," boasted Goering recently. "Our aërial and undersea fighters are taking care of our war against the British Isles. At the beginning of the conflict, England proclaimed that this war was an economic contest which industrial production would win or lose. Well, we have accepted the challenge. Britain today depends for her supplies on thousands of miles of uncertain water routes. German production is dependent only on our own strength. Our Fuehrer sits in the pilot's seat, and our workers are at their machines. We will defeat England industrially before we smash her militarily."

And the tragedy of this arrogant boast is that it is justified. Germany will win the Battle of the Atlantic, unless America stops Hitler before he reaches the Atlantic coast line of Africa.

III

ENGLAND alone against Europe cannot last.

England is fast being exhausted economically and financially. Even now she is being plunged into misery and ruin. Those who are seeking to tranquilize the American people by the consolation that time is working for the British Empire are holding up a mirage. Nay, they are playing with fire. And a devastating fire it is!

That reasassuring reference to time is the invention of parlor strategists who are, consciously or unconsciously, furthering the spirit of *laisser-aller* in America. Repeated over and over again by certain politicians and columnists, facile affirmations of that kind have the effect which Hitler rightly attributes to a lie that is restated often enough: in the end it sticks. "England loses every battle but the last." "It takes Britons a long time to get into their stride." "No matter how black the outlook at present, Britain is bound to win in the end." Platitudes such as these have contributed immensely towards fostering and preserving in the American people, for well-nigh two years, that dangerous—because paralyzing—state of mind where reality is disregarded.

Since the German invasion of Poland, Britain has received one blow after the other, until today the Empire is staggering on its feet and literally gasping for breath. Even so, the senseless game goes on of minimizing every disaster England suffers and, reversely, of magnifying such totally inconsequential military feats as the conquest of Italian East Africa. It has been made to appear, for instance, that in taking Addis Ababa the British army had captured the equivalent of the first suburb of Berlin; the victory at Asmara has been shortsightedly conceded as having the strategical importance of Genoa and Trieste combined.

The reinforcement of the Greek and Jugoslav lines by British troops in early April was hailed by a chorus of commentators as a move of surpassing importance, ushering in the turning of the tide. One particular observer, who claims the attention of millions of American newspaper readers, described it as a great British victory on a par with the withdrawal from Dunkirk and the brief British incursion into Norway—both of which events, it was conveniently forgotten, constituted disasters of the first magnitude.

Only because of an erroneous interpretation of the nature of German strategy was it possible for this argument to be advanced. It was predicated on the belief that extension of the war's area, once to Norway and since then to the Balkans, was the result of clever diplomacy or brilliant staff work on the part of the British. For are not the German lines of communication constantly lengthened? Is the Reich not being saddled with new territories to police, organize and defend, thus adding to the burdens of what is thought to be an already dangerously overtaxed German war-machine and economy?

In spite of all that has been said and written on the perversity of the Nazi mentality and the super-Machiavellianism of German diplomacy, we were taken in by Herr Hitler's violent reaction to the Jugloslav refusal to be peacefully integrated into his New Order. When he loudly blamed British and American diplomacy for Belgrade's final decision to make a stand, we fell into the trap. We failed to realize that this resistance to his

34

demands was precisely what he desired, and that in fact he had engineered matters to that end.

The same indignation was shown by the German Foreign Office when the British sent troops into Iraq. There, too, Herr Hitler wants his way. But first he fixes on Mr. Churchill the blame for extending the war.

It is not the British at all, but the Nazis who want to extend the war to an ever wider area. That, in fact, is the fundamental directive of Berlin's strategy. But, of course, Germany's expansionist intentions are to be covered with a cloak of historical and military inevitability. It is a trick which works with consistent effectiveness, a double-edged diplomatic knife that cuts both ways: Herr Hitler, we know now from many of his past performances—the Reichstag Fire, the Blood Purge of 1934, the murder of Dollfuss and other sanguinary exploits—is deeply concerned with fastening on others the responsibility for his acts.

In this case he is resolved, if he can, to hang on London and on Washington the crime of spreading the armed conflict. At least in the eyes of his own people and of an eventual peace conference, if ever such a conference should be held. In any case—that is, no matter if at such a conference a defeated Reich is summoned before its judges, or if Herr Hitler dictates the terms of peace—the argument of injured innocence can be turned to equally good account.

When Hitler protested so vehemently that no other course had been left him but to occupy Norway, Denmark, the Netherlands, Belgium and, later, Bulgaria and Jugoslavia, in order to protect those countries from a violation of their neutrality by Britain, he was not merely engaging in oratorical pyrotechnics. He was seeking to disinculpate himself before the bar of history. He was also—and that with far more immediate effect—

furnishing valuable ammunition to those isolationists in America who spread the falsehood that all of humanity's present woes must be attributed to the American government's meddling in European and international affairs—first by the President's famous quarantine speech, and later by stiffening the determination to resist of Britain, France, Jugoslavia and Greece.

The British urged the Jugoslavs to stand up and fight in the hope of bringing Turkey and, eventually, the Soviet Union into the war. It was a gamble. They are not so far bereft of common sense in Whitehall as to have ever entertained the notion that Jugoslavia and Greece alone, even with the aid of the Australian Expeditionary Force, could hold back the German warmachine, let alone create a permanent front in eastern Europe from which the Germans could eventually be driven back into Bulgaria and Rumania. Churchill took a desperate gamble in the Balkans. Even he will concede that. But it was a chance he had to take.

It has been said by his opponents that Britain's undaunted 67-year-old warrior is a reckless, impulsive gambler who refuses to listen to the advice of military experts. His expeditionary offensive moves against superior forces have been called mere invitations of disaster. But such is not the case. Churchill is a brilliant military strategic thinker. His Dardanelles campaign of 1915 and his recent Greek adventure were gambles; but they were legitimate war gambles. England's war leader has always maintained that the fate of the British Empire will be decided by a Near Eastern campaign. There was no defect in his plans to stop Hitler in Greece. His resources, however, were insufficient. He knew that he was attempting the impossible and that his chances of success were small indeed. But he would never have been forced to attempt it, if British diplomacy had not been completely outwitted or the intelligence service had not failed him. For one may now be quite sure that the wily Mr. Matsuoka—instead of being the badly disillusioned Japanese diplomat some of our newspapers pictured him to be when he learned, upon his arrival at Berlin, of Jugoslavia's determination to fight—actually served as a most efficient messenger between Berlin, Rome and Moscow. Long before the Nazis struck at Jugoslavia the Japanese Foreign Minister informed Herr Hitler that Russia, and hence Turkey, would not make a move in defense of Belgrade.

In 1941, in the Balkans, Herr Hitler again employed the artifice that had so effectively fooled Gamelin the year before; I mean the thrice-repeated concentration of German armored divisions on the Dutch and Belgian borders. Twice Gamelin rose to the bait and revealed to the German General Staff what his strategy would be in the event of an attack in those quarters. Each time he rushed forward beyond his defense lines, thus exposing the French forces. When the Germans, after two feints, really struck, the French were laid open to a piercing thrust in the plains of Flanders, Artois and Champagne, where they had made no preparations whatsoever. By starting hostilities against Jugoslavia, Germany lured the best part of Wavell's glorious army away from the scene of its victories in Egypt and Libya.

Far from being an act of desperation to prevent the British from creating an Eastern front, or a hurried counter-stroke to a daring British initiative, the German drive into the Balkans was a carefully executed, perfectly timed detail of their master-plan. The notion that the British, at least, did upset Hitler's spring schedule was absurd. Hitler, not Britain, timed the attack on Jugoslavia and Greece.

For months on end Berlin allowed Britain and the

world to cherish the illusion that the Italian Axis partner could be knocked out of the war. At one time, in
the early spring, rumors were rife that Italy was about
to sue for peace and that Italian diplomats were on their
way to London to sound out Winston Churchill on the
prospect of a separate armistice. The Italian attack on
Greece was made to appear as a reckless adventure un-
dertaken by a Duce disgruntled over the small amount
of booty he had received after the fall of France. Dispatch after dispatch told of an ever-widening rift
between the German and Italian dictators over the invasion of Greece. Ingenious publicists gave us descrip-
tions of what was happening in the most secret con-
ferences of the German High Command, even as we had
for long been reading what Adolf Hitler muttered to
himself when he put on his night cap or what battles
were raging in the subconscious recesses of his brain,
which had contemptuously been adjudicated the mind
of a megalomanaic.

Hitler was said to be deliberately letting Mussolini
ruin himself, punishing the Duce, as it were, for not
consulting the German High Command prior to the
invasion of Greece. On the other hand, Hitler's Polish,
Scandinavian and French laurels were said to be leaving
Mussolini no rest. He too wanted his share of glory. So
at least it was said.

Only when the Italian campaign in Albania turned
into disaster and the Italian armies were rolled back in
Libya and Ethiopia, did Hitler relent and finally come
to the aid of his hard-pressed partner.

Why had the Fuehrer, a commander with 250 divisions idle on his hands, waited till the last hour, until
Mussolini seemed at his wit's end and with his back to
the wall?

The answer is that, in the first place, the Fuehrer had

obtained the satisfaction of seeing the British disperse their weak forces over several widely separated theatres of war. Instead of reinforcing their hopelessly inadequate garrisons in Palestine and thus preventing a pro-Axis *coup d'état* in Iraq, the British had thrown away their advantage for a cheap victory in the Ethiopian wildlands. They had, moreover, done exactly what the Fuehrer had wanted them to do, in that they had depleted Wavell's army of its already dangerously insufficient mechanized equipment in Egypt. Instead of the British fleet and air force attacking the Italian gun emplacements and the new German airdrome on the microscopic island of Pantelleria, halfway between Sicily and the African mainland, the Royal navy had been employed in convoying troop ships to Piraeus. The result was that one day a section of the Italian fleet was able to come out and serve as a decoy in the Ionian Sea—to be attacked and partly destroyed by the British —while the bulk of the *panzer* equipment was quietly ferried across from Italy to Libya for a new Axis drive on the Suez Canal.

In less than a month's time the Jugoslav and Greek defense crumbled, the British army in Greece was lost, Wavell's drive to Cyrenaica was nullified. Turkey had become isolated and ready for diplomatic and military pressure, Iraq, with the Mosul oil fields, had been brought within Hitler's sight, and the Suez Canal was caught between the prongs of a gigantic pincer.

At the beginning of May the British army was standing in the semi-arch that runs from Haifa to Alexandria, with its back to the Red Sea, hoping for a swift termination of the Ethiopian campaign, looking for reinforcements from Australia and India (at a moment when Japan had just had her hands freed in the Pacific by Comrade Stalin), waiting for Danish ships with material from America—ships which were, at best, two months away.

At the same time, General Franco, with the aid of German engineers, had been quietly fortifying the Canary Islands and laying out airdromes and constructing submarine bases at Algeciras and on the island of Majorca. He had also handed Tangier over to the Germans, allowed tens of thousands of German soldiers into Spanish Morocco and other tens of thousands into southern Spain. Thus were the approaches of the Straits of Gibraltar turned into an armed camp, with Franco awaiting the hour of arrival of the first German mechanized troops at Port Said, the eastern door of the Mediterranean, before himself closing the western gateway to that sea, in order to trap British naval units operating there.

The Axis would never have inaugurated the military phase of the Mediterranean battle in its eastern corner without first having secured complete control over its western entrance. This was done early in 1939 by the defeat of the Spanish Republic at the hands of General Franco, who operated as an agent of the Axis powers. When "peace" was reëstablished in Spain by the conquest of Madrid it meant, translated into military terms, that Hitler had won the preliminary skirmish in the Mediterranean battle. Franco handed the key to the western gate of the Mediterranean to the Fuehrer in return for Axis aid in stamping out Communism.

The amazing aspect of this prelude to the great Mediterranean drama is that the British General Staff was fully aware of the disastrous significance of Spain's passing into the control of Hitler. In April, 1938, Captain Liddell Hart, noted military expert, sent to Mr. Hore-Belisha, British Secretary of State for War, a memorandum wherein, among other things, he said:

"The military key to the whole [European] situation lies in Spain. As I have been pointing out for eighteen months, a German-Italian domination of Spain would place heavy odds against the success of Britain and France in a war with these powers. Any one must be blind who cannot see that a victory now for Franco spells this domination. Militarily it has been much easier for us to prevent that victory than for Germany and Italy to secure it. The cards are still in our hands—until Franco and his allies secure the eastern seaboard of Spain. When that happens the whole game is likely to be lost.

"The growth in the speed and range of modern weapons, especially aircraft, has made the Mediterranean Sea strategically a 2,000-mile 'canal'—from Port Said to Gibraltar. A significant feature of the last war was the high percentage of commerce destruction that was achieved in the Mediterranean in proportion to the small forces employed in the submarine campaign there —there were rarely more than half a dozen submarines operating at any one time. A single one of them attained a total 'bag' of half a million tons of shipping. German naval histories have dwelt on the 'extraordinary possibilities' offered by operations in the Mediterranean. Yet the campaign was carried on at an immense distance from the home bases of the submarines and under the great difficulties caused by the hazardous passage past the British Isles and the lack of convenient bases in the Mediterranean.

"Nowadays, submarines have multiplied; new types of high-speed torpedo-craft have been developed; and the range of aircraft has been vastly extended. Moreover, we are now confronted with the ominous possibility that, if Italy should be an enemy, these menaces to sea traffic could operate from bases close to the traffic routes.

41

It would be worse still if Spain were ranged on the opposing side, and her bases, both sea and air, were available for the enemy's use. For Spain, through her geographical position, forms the lock gates at the west end of the 'Mediterranean Canal.'

"We ought to be clear what this would mean. In the first place, Gibraltar would be untenable as a naval base. The anchorage there is narrow, as the sea-floor shelves sharply, and could not be used by our ships if it were under fire from hostile guns on the Spanish shore. A few mobile batteries, suddenly brought there, would suffice to make it unusable. We should then be left with no secure naval base of our own between this country and Alexandria, over 3,000 miles distant. In comparison with this fact, it is a secondary question whether our ships would be able to pass through the Straits of Gibraltar into, and out of, the Mediterranean. None the less, the mere possibility that air and naval bases on the eastern seaboard of Spain and in the Balearic Isles might be available for our opponents' use seriously complicates the problem of maintaining our traffic through, or even our forces in, the Mediterranean. It is at least an equal danger to the communications between France and her African colonies.

"Nor does the risk end there. The alternative route to the East round the Cape, and even the sea approaches to this country, would be jeopardized from the north-western and southwestern coasts of Spain. And this threat would be extended by an enemy's use of the Canary Isles. Thus, from a strategical point of view, the political outcome of the present struggle is not, and cannot be, a matter of indifference to us. A friendly Spain is desirable, a neutral Spain is vital."

The occupation of Greece places both Egypt and Palestine—that is, the British naval base at Alexandria and the British naval fueling station at Haifa, which is the terminus of the Mosul pipe-line—within easy reach of German land-based bombers. Independently with a resumed German-Italian drive by mechanized columns from Libya and another German drive through Turkey, Syria and Palestine, the British position in Egypt will become utterly hazardous in the course of the summer of 1941 by reason of the bombing menace alone. Hitherto naval units have given land-based bombers a wide berth; there is no reason to hope that this will be any different in the future. German bombers stationed in Greece will have for their task the smashing of Britain's bases in the eastern Mediterranean and driving the British navy out of that corner of the Old World Sea. In the latter part of 1940 German newspapers were announcing that the coming summer would witness "the history-changing spectacle of the British policeman ignominiously being driven from Italy's *Lebensraum*."

It is quite possible that before the overland drives toward the Suez Canal get under way, the Germans may make an attempt to capture or render totally impotent the strategic island of Malta. For Malta, strongest of Britain's naval and aërial *points d'appui* in the Mediterranean, lies athwart Italy's lines of communication with North Africa. Could the island's airdromes and naval station be destroyed, the flow of war material and men to the Italo-German army in Libya would no longer be interfered with and the investment of Egypt not much longer delayed.

A possibility to be reckoned with, though not a likely one, is that Turkey may procrastinate about affording passage to a German army bent on the seizure of the Mosul oil fields. In that event, the execution of an alternative plan would be attempted, for Hitler is seeking to avoid a conflict with Turkey. Were Turkey to

stand firm, Germany's Libyan army would seek to continue its march through Egypt, across the Canal, through
Sinai and Palestine and out from there to Mosul. There
is no doubt, though, that the great battle which will
decide the fate of the British Empire will be fought out
in the triangle of Alexandria-Haifa-Basra.

IV

THE assumption that the Battle of the Atlantic is the pivot upon which world history turns is false. Britain as an empire stands or falls with the control of the Near East. Once the Mediterranean basin passes into German hands, the British Empire is broken in two and a process of disintegration sets in that will leave of the British Empire nothing but a ravaged little island exhausted by hunger, its cities and ports mere heaps of rubble.

Now, what would be Hitler's most logical moves if, after the fall of Suez and Gibraltar, the British government does not succumb to the new wave of appeasement bound to arise both in England and in America, and instead decides to fight on?

First there would be a lull in the land operations to consolidate conquered positions in the Near and Middle East, reconstruct and reorientate bases of operation, repair oil wells, collect stocks, build roads and lay out new airdromes. But that interval would not mean a breathing spell for England herself. Britain would be subjected to continuous and intensive mass-bombardment. And the trans-Atlantic shipping lanes, to which then will have been added the traffic routes along the West Coast of Africa—that is to say, England's only remaining road to the Far East—would be exposed to "the wolf packs of submarines" Admiral Raeder gathered together during the winter and spring. (This, of course, assumes that the United States will adhere to the maxim of "all aid to Britain short of war," which is tantamount to a warrant for Hitler to continue with impunity his disastrous raids on British shipping.)

The interruption of land operations in the Near East would perhaps last till the beginning of the autumn of 1941. Then the drive would be resumed and a new stage, a new interlude, in the German master-plan would be ushered in. On separate dates, or simultaneously, German-Italian mechanized columns would strike south through the Sudan and Kenya, bent on the conquest of the former German colony of Tanganyika, and an army would be embarked at Port Said, Ishmaila and Suez for the reconquest of Eritrea and Ethiopia, where there would be no British army to assist Haile Selassie in his defense. For that army would have been used up in the defense of Egypt and contiguous areas.

But Ethiopia is not the final objective in Germany's African drive. The goal is Cape Town and the Union of South Africa. Following the trail made by the South Africans, who marched to Italian Somaliland in the early months of 1941, the Germans will stage a repetition of the Sudetenland farce when they reach the borders of the South African dominion. Their coming has long been announced in Windhoek and Pretoria as the signal for the final liberation of the Boer minority from the British yoke. This being the Reich's pretended motive for the invasion of South Africa, the country would most likely be thrown into confusion and civil turmoil long before the mechanized columns appear on the veldt's horizon.

For it is a matter of record that in the course of the Ethiopian campaign, during the early months of 1941, the political atmosphere in South Africa was so charged with explosive possibilities that Premier Jan Christian Smuts dared not leave the capital but for a few brief and secret visits to the firing line. Once martial law had to be proclaimed in the overwhelmingly Dutch province of Transvaal, and an incipient uprising of back-veldt elements in Johannesburg had to be quelled by troops.

Three times since the start of the war, too, General Herzog, the leader of the nationalist Boer opposition, has introduced a motion in Parliament calling for "an immediate termination" of the state of war with Germany into which South Africa, "against her will and best interests," has been "dragged" by "the imperial connexion." The motion was defeated by a significantly small majority. And in April, 1941, the Synod of the Dutch Reformed Church in session at Pietermaritzburg, in order to make it clear that with the Boers it is not a question of being rather more anti-British than pro-German, came out openly for the Nazi philosophy, even going to the extent of rebuking certain pastors in Holland who had condemned Hitlerism as anti-Christian. This rebuke came simultaneously with a belated expression of satisfaction over the defeat of France, for that country had committed the sin—unpardonable in the eyes of the South African Calvinists—of having placed native African troops on a footing of equality with white soldiers and of having used them in the defense of the republic.

The German propaganda department, which has for years shown a deep interest in the anti-British sentiment prevalent amongst the irreconcilable Boers, lately gave new impetus to that spirit by making it known in South Africa that the most elaborate film to be turned out by the Reich's studios in the course of 1941 would have the title *Oom Paul Kruger*. In this film, which will portray the war of 1899-1900 between England and the Boer Republics, Britain will be shown as the initiator of the concentration camp for civilian prisoners and women. The smart of that epoch, still rankling in the

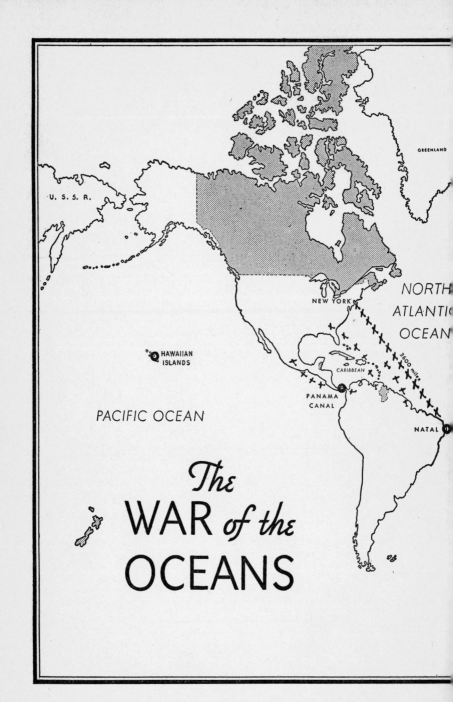

The WAR of the OCEANS

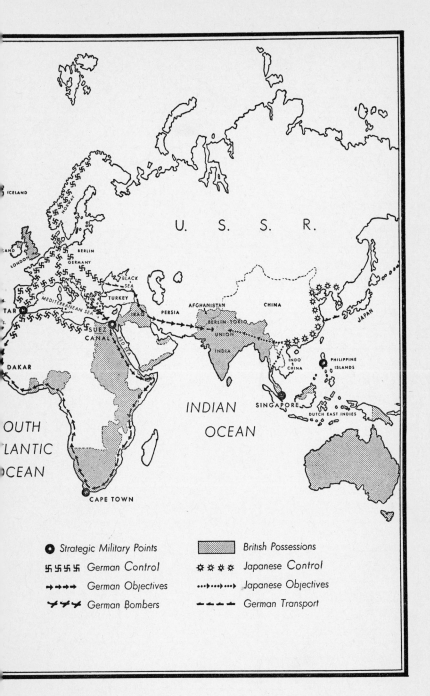

ICELAND

U. S. S. R.

NORWAY

BERLIN
GERMANY

LONDON

BLACK
SEA

TURKEY

AFGHANISTAN   CHINA

JAPAN

MEDITERRANEAN SEA

IRAQ   PERSIA

BERLIN-TOKIO

TAR

SUEZ
CANAL

LIBYA

UNION

INDIA

INDO
CHINA

PHILIPPINE
ISLANDS

DAKAR

INDIAN

OCEAN

SINGAPORE

DUTCH EAST INDIES

OUTH
LANTIC
CEAN

CAPE TOWN

⊙ Strategic Military Points

卐 卐 卐 German Control

→→→→ German Objectives

✈✈✈ German Bombers

British Possessions

✿ ✿ ✿ Japanese Control

••▸••▸••▸ Japanese Objectives

-- -- -- German Transport

hearts of the young Boers because it has so constantly been fed by bitter, unforgiving Calvinist rhetoric in the pulpits, is at last to be assuaged by the ousting of the British "usurpers."

Smuts will fight like a lion when the hour comes. But the Boers will have their Quisling in some man like Pirow, who was a minister in Herzog's cabinet and who —so the German press announced proudly in 1938, when he paid a visit to the Fuehrer—once declared: "At home I speak only German, because that is my mother tongue, of which no one can rob me; but I also pray for the day when the hated English language shall no longer be heard in the whole length and breadth of our continent."

With both the longitudinal African coast lines under German domination, from Suez to Cape Town and from Cape Town to Dakar and Tangier, it will not be long before circumnavigation of the Cape of Good Hope by British ships on their way to and from the Far East and India will become fraught with risks too great to take.

The war would then logically move into the Western hemisphere. For England's only remaining access to the antipodal dominions would be through the Panama Canal and the Straits of Magellan.

In the Middle East Germany will proceed with the execution of the next step of her plan for world conquest, which will most probably be launched simultaneously with the drive into Africa. The Nazi legions will move from Iraq into Persia.

Persia is not expected to offer much resistance, the more so since the Soviet Union is there slated to repeat the treachery it practiced in the case of Poland, by stabbing Persia in the back.

In modern times the Kingdom of Persia has been more

or less of a geographical expression divided into two spheres of interest. First the Czars and later the Soviets have held the northern part under their economic control, and the southern part, where the properties of the Anglo-Persian Oil Company are located, has been supervised by Britain. The Anglo-Persian Company maintains a private army for the protection of its valuable properties. A few years ago, when the new Shah, Reza Khan, protested against the presence of that foreign army in his domains and threatened to expel it, British destroyers came dashing up the Persian Gulf and quickly brought the man on the Peacock Throne to reason.

Germany will promise the Shah to throw out the British and guarantee him his throne, on the condition that he cedes the northern provinces of Iran to the Soviet Union. This because Russia must be placated for the prospective loss of another sphere of influence—in Afghanistan, for Afghanistan is a focal objective in Germany's eastward drive.

At this point an old acquaintance of the American newspaper reader makes a sensational comeback: King Amanullah! That gentleman has for years been residing in Rome. He lost his throne in 1929. He had been on a visit to the Western capitals, and was just contemplating an extension of his tour from London to New York—the steamship tickets had already been purchased—when news reached him of a revolt in Kabul. One story attributed the revolt to British agents, in retaliation for Amanullah's short-lived invasion of British India during the last war. The point has never been satisfactorily cleared up. Although it is true that the late Colonel T. E. Lawrence, who reportedly was in charge of the rebellious movement in Afghanistan, formally denied the allegation, it is also true that this brilliant guerrilist did not die of fibbing. Once when the newspapers reported him to be serving in the air force or to be tinkering with speedboats in the harbor of Southampton, I found him in the home of Mr. St. John Philby, the British Near Eastern agent in Djedda.

The plain and simple fact is that Amanullah wants his throne back. In April, 1941, his host, Signor Mussolini, furnished him with a passport so that he might discuss the matter with Herr Hitler in Berlin. The king was referred to the Department of Oriental Affairs in the Wilhelmstrasse, according to the *Voelkische Beobachter*, and later had dinner with Marshal Goering. The communiqué stated that Amanullah and the German authorities reached a complete harmony of views.

Germany will, therefore, have the pretext of entering Afghanistan to set aright an ancient wrong committed by the wicked English. Nor will she fail to publish her noble intention of restoring Amanullah on his throne. German troops will also remain to see him safely installed—for Afghanistan is the gateway to India.

India!

What political situation Germany may be able to exploit in India when her mechanized legions are standing at the Khyber Pass no one can foretell. The Hindu people will certainly not be eager to exchange British rule, which they know, for German mastery, which they do not know by actual experience but of which they have heard enough. They might even be stirred from the lethargy into which their extreme poverty has plunged them, and might rally to Britain's side in a *levée en masse*. But the essential condition for such a move would appear to be Britain's definite promise and guarantees that self-government would be their reward. This the Tories of England are not likely to grant any more than they accepted the offer of Jewry to raise an army for the defense of Palestine.

The chief danger to India in these circumstances, however, will be the proximity of the Japanese army in Indo-China and Thailand, and the obvious intention of the Axis powers to effect a juncture of their military forces before moving south to attack the Singapore base from the rear.

That would ring down the curtain on the British Empire with the "vital Atlantic sector" assumedly not yet affected.

After that there would still be an England, to be sure, but an England cut off, and without that empire for the defense of which the peoples of the British Commonwealth of Nations are now at war. In other words, there would be nothing left to defend but the bomb-battered, starved British Isles, where human life would fast become impossible.

Will it come to this? Does the German plan seem too fantastic? Will the Axis economy stand the strain of such a gigantic military enterprise? Will not the occupied countries revolt against German domination? May not a great lassitude become manifest in the German people themselves under aërial bombardment as the Fuehrer and his armies wander always farther away from home in pursuit of the dream of Alexander and Napoleon?

Consider first that the stepping-stones for that march to India have been put into place and that Hitler, once the Near East is in his power, will have frustrated the British blockade to the extent that he will no longer lack oil and other raw materials. Food will be plentiful too, with the granaries of eastern Europe and of Egypt at his command.

It is an illusion to think or hope that Russia will intervene somewhere on Hitler's march to the East. To judge by the record of the last two years, the task of Russia, that silent power in the Axis—*n'en déplaise messieurs les communistes*—has been to give comfort and consolation to the master in Berlin by her valuable passive attitude and her more than benevolent "neutrality." Germany's geopolitical planners advised Herr Hitler long ago not to attack Russia—this on the grounds that Russia as a Soviet state had performed a useful function for Nazi Germany by withholding one sixth of the earth's habitable surface from plutocratic exploitation and thus undermining and weakening capitalist economy in the whole world. During the Balkan campaign, Joseph and his brethren in the Kremlin, petrified with fear of Hitler, obligingly covered Adolf's left flank. In compensation they were allowed to take Bessarabia—which the Communist totalitarians interpreted as a matter of improving the Soviet's defense positions. It may well have been a precautionary move against the well-known aggressive intentions of the Montenegrin peasants or the gypsies of Wallachia.

However that may be, the New Germany thinks in terms of continental strategy. Old England's permanent policy was to keep an artificial balance of power in Europe, which *ipso facto* safeguarded her colonial holdings. Hitler's Reich has always been intent on new conquests; Chamberlain's Britain aimed to maintain the *status quo*. Hence Germany has for the last eight years been politically and militarily on the march, unburdened by tradition or responsibilities or wealth, while England was afraid to move because it might precipitate a change. Nazi diplomacy was flexible, revolutionary, unscrupulous, ready to change direction at any time and even to reverse itself completely.

Number 10 Downing Street, no less than the Geopolitical Institute in Munich, has always known that Russia's interests in Europe are purely passive and defensive. Of the territories she seized on her western frontiers in the course of the present war—parts of Poland and Rumania, Lithuania, Latvia and Esthonia, and military bases in Finland—almost all once constituted part of the Czar's domains. England, however, did not relish the idea of an invulnerable Russia, any more than she favored a strong France. It is no wonder, therefore, that England lost out on the Soviet Union issue. She had to lose, unless she was willing to risk some of her holdings in the East.

British politicians realized that Soviet security in the West meant that the Kremlin would thenceforward look toward the East.

The Soviet Union, now that Hitler is marching eastward, stands on the threshold of what was Czarist Russia's most ambitious imperialist objective: India. Only in that vast and populous area does Moscow expect to receive its full reward for the pact with Germany. Had Hitler not undone General Wavell's victory in the Near East, Stalin would not have drunk that ludicrous toast with Matsuoka to the health of the Japanese Emperor. But with German troops opening a path to India, Russia now more than ever will maintain a pro-German policy. Unless Hitler, if he reaches Iran and Afghanistan, refuses Stalin his share of the booty, Moscow is committed to an even closer relationship with Berlin. Their interests do not clash. They supplement each other. Both desire the collapse of the British Empire. Russia, with more than three quarters of her territory on the Asiatic continent, is content and prepared to see the emergence of a Nazified Europe, which she pretends to fear no more than a British-dominated Europe. The non-aggression pact between Stalin and Hitler will never be broken unless Hitler wills it. To hope that the Red Army will clash with Hitler's *panzer* divisions before Britain is defeated is to cherish an illusion.

Consider, too, the false ideas about the Arab world. I mean the quiet expectation nursed in certain quarters that Britain may count on the unqualified support of King Ibn Saoud, the Imam of Yemen, the Emir of Transjordania and other Arabic princes and chieftains, if and when it comes to a last extremity in the British defense of the Near East. There are people who sincerely believe that if Britain's position in the Near and Middle East should really grow desperate it will take only a signal from some secret British agent to set the entire Arabic world aflame. Somewhere between Sana and Basra, they fondly imagine, sits another young Englishman of the caliber of T. E. Lawrence who holds all the strings in his hands. At a given moment they expect him to manipulate all the internecine Arabic intrigues in such a manner that vast hordes of wild Arabic cavalry will come careening through the desert, blowing up supply columns, darting hither and yon to harass, ambush and hack to pieces straggling units of the invader.

There is no greater illusion than that picture of romance and magic. It should not be forgotten, in the first place, that in order to win the tribes for his "Revolt in the Desert" in 1917 Lawrence had engaged in long months of negotiation, bribery and palaver. And he had a definite goal to hold out: loot, and liberation from the Turkish yoke. When he once quietly mentioned, to a group of Arab chiefs gathered in Feisal's tent on the shore of the Red Sea, that Akaba was a long way from Damascus, "a shudder ran through the assembly." That shudder was the nervous anticipation of men eager for a great looting expedition. In the present state of affairs, Britain can hold out to the Arabs nothing but sweat and blood and tears.

It may be objected that although the Arab principalities do not dispose of any modern military establishments and although the Arabs have for centuries shown themselves bereft of genuine fighting qualities they could still be used as guerrillists and irregulars.

The answer to this is that they have not shown the slightest disposition to rally to Britain's side in the present conflict. To the contrary! We can see the attitude of the King and government of Egypt, who have let the British do all the fighting in Libya—and even inside invaded Egyptian territory!—without so much as raising a finger in support of their protectors. In Iraq, again, there has been the pro-Axis *coup d'état* engineered by Rashid Ali Beg Galiani. Does this not furnish Britain and the world with a pretty accurate index of what is in the wind in that quarter? As soldiers, the Arabs may be left out of consideration; but as cutthroats and backstabbers the tribes can do a fearful amount of harm to an already inadequate force operating in their habitat and fighting with its back to the wall.

Rashid Ali Beg Galiani is the Quisling of Iraq. He seized power over the Mosul oil fields even before the arrival of the Germans, whose financial and propaganda agents prepared him for the job of giving Britain an unexpected blow from an unexpected quarter the moment the position of her army in the Near East should grow critical. He struck while Britain was fighting the desperate Battle of Greece. Subsequently, when he discovered that his coup had been premature, Galiani declared, in effect, that he intended to uphold the Anglo-Iraq treaty—a statement on a par with General Franco's protestations that he did not intend to let German troops march into Spain. The fact remains that Galiani did seize power, and that Franco did let in an advance guard of 35,000 German soldiers as far back as February, 1941 (ostensibly to help in clearing the hurricane ruins of Santander, a task apparently beyond the capacities of Spain's two million unemployed).

Even the British discarded Galiani's protestations of loyalty. The London *Times* wrote that "the serious upset in Iraq" was the work of the exiled Mufti of Jerusalem, Ai Hameen el Husseini, a murdering, illiterate intrigant who should have been hanged long ago.

In Syria another revolt took place, ostensibly against the French government, but in fact directed against Britain. The proof of this is that the revolt was incited, supported and financed by German and Italian agents, ably assisted by that same Mufti of Jerusalem. It was this Mufti who instigated a blood bath in Palestine in 1929.

It is for the sake of this Ai Hameen el Husseini, to win his support and approval of British control in the Middle East, that the British government has systematically blocked and undermined Zionist efforts and Jewish aspirations in Palestine. The ex-Mufti launched his violent anti-Jewish and anti-British policy as far back as 1920, when he organized the first massacre of Jews in Jerusalem. For this service to humanity he was appointed President of the Supreme Moslem Council, while the organizer of Jewish self-defense, Vladimir Jabotinsky, received a fifteen-year prison sentence. Jabotinsky had wanted to defend not only the Jews but the very principle of the British mandate over Palestine, under which the Jews are in their ancient homeland by right and by international sanction.

Through nearly twenty years of pogroms, revolts, sabotage and intrigues Ai Hameen el Husseini rose to a position of power and influence throughout the Middle East—with the blessings of the Colonial Office and with a fine salary paid from the Palestine treasury. In 1941 he started paying England back in full. The Jews, on the other hand, relying on the solemn pledge of the British government to facilitate their task in building a homeland, saw their hopes frustrated by successive British administrations, which curtailed immigration on one pretext or another, placed restrictions on land sales, even turned back Jewish children fleeing from the Hitler terror, and in the end refused a Jewish offer to recruit an army in Palestine.

Why?

Because until the Empire cracked on its foundations, British statesmen continued to toy with the idea of an Arab federation and of Arab sympathies. That toying, which involved a flagrant breach of faith with the Jewish people and with the nations that had ratified Britain's mandate over Palestine, in the end deprived Great Britain of a solid bastion of modern Maccabees stationed on the shores of the Suez Canal and ready to hurl themselves against the Nazi legions in the hour of the Empire's anguish.

But even in that hour a die-hard Tory like Lord Halifax—who ought to know that a Christian's first duty is penitence—refused to admit the grievous blunder of his government and the cruel imposition on the hardest-pressed people on earth. Instead, he asserted that Britain had always done her full duty by the Jewish people.

V

Interpreters of the war have hailed every lull in the more spectacular phases of Nazi military activity as a symptom of Germany's approaching collapse. They began with the period of seven long months which elapsed between Hitler's conquest of Poland and the invasion of Norway, and repeated with unfailing regularity thereafter whenever Hitler paused in his march of conquest. On each occasion, whether it was after the collapse of France or after the overrunning of Rumania, we were told that Hitler was now out of breath or that we could calmly look forward to a gradual deterioration of the Nazi power.

What do the geopoliticians say about these interludes? Their answer, given in 1941, is: "Germany has not yet reached the acme of her strength. . . . Germany will not improvise the last passage-at-arms, but will prepare everything with Prussian exactitude. . . . No time is being wasted. . . . *Germany waits quickly.* . . . The tempo of waiting is determined by men"—note the use of the term "men" instead of the name "Hitler"—"who constantly demand the utmost, that which is just within the limits of possibility. Germany is using her waiting time to gain her full strength. England is using up all her strength to gain time. That is one great difference. The other is that Germany is waiting on her own account, determining the time for the unleashing of the decisive assault, as well as for every other action; England is waiting for the enemy, and must submit to his choice of the hour and form of conflict."

We should, therefore, not be deluded when after—or even before—the fall of Suez, Gibraltar and Malta, an apparent inactivity on the part of the German war-machine sets in. Such an interlude will occur—and it will mean the taking of a running start for a particularly broad jump. "Every apparent inactivity and every impending action serves the sole purpose of imparting the greatest possible force to the decisive blow against England." Thus the Geopolitical Institute speaks to its disciples in the German General Staff when they grow restless and impatient with the long periods of preparation.

"Hitler must strike now if he is to strike at all" is another of the facile and even dangerous phrases of our too optimistic commentators. I call it dangerous because it has no relationship to a true evaluation of the time element in this war of the oceans, which after two years of fighting is still in its initial stage.

Europe, now completely dominated by the Nazis, may enjoy a "perfect Nazi peace" enforced by the Gestapo, while the German armies are engaged in the war of the oceans. In other words, Hitler's planners foresee the possibility of carrying on simultaneously the consolidation of a Nazi-unified "peace" economy in Europe and a wide-scope military action in other parts of the world. This prospect of a permanent war of conquest the Nazis do not, as peaceful people would, regard as a nightmare, but rather as an ideal. The masters are to be the knights of battle, while the subject nations slave and provide prosperity and luxuries for the German people. For subjection to the Nazis means collaboration, whether enforced as in the case of Holland, Scandinavia and France, or voluntary as in the case of Hungary, Rumania and Italy.

A total peace, according to the saber-rattling philosophers of Nazidom, brings decadence and demoralization to a virile race. Victorious campaigns on foreign territory are desirable at all times and should take the place of the old-time army maneuvers, to keep the nation-in-arms in constant trim. Casualties can be reduced to a minimum by an even more perfected mechanization of war tactics. But war must go on, the ideologists of the New Order agree: that, and not peace, is the Nordic's normal estate.

It is quite imperative for us to understand Hitler's long-range views about the war. For unless we do, we are apt to continue to live in a world of illusions until it is too late. There is, it must be said without regard for personalities, too much loose talk about what Hitler intends or does not intend to do, by people who have not even the faintest notion of the most elementary aspects of the scope of Hitler's war of the oceans. Far too often the "low-down" on the international situation is given us in the vernacular of sports writers estimating the relative strength of two prize fighters. Characteristic of such "inside news" is a little item which appeared, at the time of the British retreat in Greece, in the New York *Daily News* by one of Broadway's experts on foreign affairs. Said this straight-from-the-Stork-Club broadcaster: "Hitler plans to end the war after conquering the Balkans, according to an amazing tip received in Washington. The Nazi armies will continue to police all the conquered countries, but refuse to fight unless the British insist on it. In this way, he [Hitler] will pass the buck to England and the United States for continuing the war, and by the same ruse keep Russia and Turkey out of it."

Here we have a typical example of irresponsible confusion-mongering and of anesthetizing American public opinion. It is tantamount to denying the incontrovertible fact of the reality of Hitler's campaign for world conquest. And it implies, of course—no, it says outright —that Hitler is content to leave England alone and to rest on his laurels for the remainder of his days. There is no further need for aid to Britain, therefore; no necessity for an American defense program. Hitler is calling the war off. Our worries are over.

No wonder President Roosevelt complains that the American people are not aware of the gravity of the situation.

When Mr. Roosevelt said, in April, that the situation is more dangerous than the American people imagine, he did not refer particularly to the hazardous position of the Greek and British armies in the Balkans or even to Great Britain's condition, which was indeed even then so critical that no one had any more doubts on the subject. The President spoke of America's position. Nor was he philosophizing about some indeterminate time in the future or speculating on circumstances that might possibly arise should certain eventualities, now still vague and distant, actually come to pass. He had in mind the concrete and immediate peril hanging over the American people's heads in the spring of 1941.

Now, on the face of it, such a declaration by the Chief of State, uttered with the greatest solemnity, should, one would think, have produced a profound shock throughout the country. The more so since reports on the progress of America's rearmament program, issued almost simultaneously with the President's warning, were on the whole quite favorable. Even so, Mr. Roosevelt's pronouncement caused hardly a ripple in the land. And yet the President is not an alarmist, and least of all a pessimist. Few will deny that Mr. Roosevelt today finds himself face to face with a crisis the evolution of which will fix his place and the place of this country in history, for better or for worse, for a long time to come. A crisis of such magnitude as has never before confronted the American people, not even in 1776 or in 1861. Mr. Roosevelt, who had all the data before him, who knew the full extent of the hour's gravity, was therefore not likely to have engaged in idle chatter or to have been playing the bogeyman.

Yet here in America I felt the people's unconcern and downright apathy to be strangely—nay, harrowingly— reminiscent of the days in France in 1939 and 1940. In that country, too, people were still shrugging their shoulders when the enemy had already thrown all caution to the winds and had, in fact, most effectively disrupted France's carefully constructed system of alliances. Czechoslovakia had been surrendered and Poland had fallen. Of what importance was that to the Parisian suburbanite who was anxious to catch the six o'clock train for Chatou-Croissy? Hadn't France the Maginot Line and the best army in the world? The French government was urging vigilance and warning of the hard blows to come. Did that mean one had to content oneself with one less *apertif* before dinner? Was not England's powerful navy mobilized in the North Sea? Was not the King of Italy certain to refuse to sanction his Duce if he made any hostile moves against France?

Warnings upon warnings were issued by those in a position to know the perilous condition of France. They fell on deaf ears, or were contemptuously dismissed as sly propaganda aimed at lowering the standard of living and at placing restrictions on civil liberties. Many fought the government's decrees tooth and nail, and in the end obstructed the national rearmament program in the belief that the danger of war was a pretext—and rearmament the instrument—of the upper classes to foist an authoritarian political régime on the country. In France they were so busy defending democracy at home, mostly by talking and writing about it, that they did not realize that with the construction of the Siegfried Line, Adolf Hitler had virtually placed a tombstone on their country.

The French people saw no overt act of hostility in the creation of a new army by Hitler. They refused to be alarmed by the *Anschluss* with Austria; they could not be persuaded that the remilitarization of the Rhineland constituted an immediate menace to French security. They failed to understand that what Hitler had captured without shedding a drop of blood were strategical positions of the most vital importance, upon the retention of which—even if some of them were at a relatively great distance from the French borders—depended a successful defense of the nation itself if war should break out. They did not realize until it was too late that the reoccupation of the Rhineland in 1937—at which time they could discern what were at the worst a few negligible cloudlets on the horizon—was in fact the guarantee of Hitler's victory in 1940. For the reoccupation by Germany of the right bank of the Rhine cut off France from her friends in eastern Europe as effectively as the capture of the Mediterranean basin will drive a wedge between North America and its potential allies in South America. From the moment German troops marched into Cologne in 1937, Czechoslovakia, Poland, Rumania, Jugoslavia, the Soviet Union and France herself were isolated militarily, and thereafter could be dealt with separately by Hitler in such a manner and at such intervals as he and his General Staff deemed propitious.

The prospect of Britain's defeat is contemplated by American isolationists with the same unconcern as was the surrender of Czechoslovakia by the appeasers of London and Paris. They speak and write of the possibility of an Empire's disappearance, an eventuality

65

which would shake the world of man to its very foundations, as if it were a matter of as little importance as a change from hanging to electrocution for convicted murderers. Empires come and empires go—perhaps not quite as fast as ice-cream cones on a hot summer's afternoon—and Britain's turn has come at last. So what? What does that matter to us? We're still safe, aren't we? England is being tossed like a ship in a tempest and the water is pouring in at the portholes, the masts are going overboard one by one and the rudder is creaking with ill-boding portent. What of it? If the ship is sinking, it merely means it's time for America to call back the lifeboat. We are told that aid to England has become superfluous and useless. Let us from now on husband our resources, instead of foolishly dumping them into Davy Jones's locker. Let us mind our own business and not go meddling into other people's affairs. Let us instead build up our defenses and be ready and strong, so that Hitler, if ever he turns his eyes in the direction of the Western hemisphere, will see there a bastion so powerful that it will rob him of all lust to engage in any further adventures.

But, then, we are also reassured, it isn't likely that he will ever dare to bother us. In the first place, it will take him years and years to consolidate his gains in Europe, Africa and Asia. He will have plenty of trouble on his hands. It will take quite some time to enslave peoples like the Britons and Greeks and Scandinavians, and swing them to his views. And, besides, is the man who could not cross the twenty-six miles of the English Channel likely to find a way to transport a mechanized army across an ocean that is three thousand miles wider? It simply cannot be done, that's all. There aren't ships enough in the world to do the job. Fly across? But we just took Greenland and deprived him of that possible

66

base for aërial attack. And, furthermore, no country has ever been conquered from the air alone.

So runs the argument, as precious time slips by and Hitler marches around the Mediterranean and gears his mechanized forces to ride around the Atlantic.

I was once a guest at Goering's home, together with several other foreign correspondents. It was in December, 1932. The Nazis had not yet come to power. But Goering felt certain, as did most of those present, that Hitler's day of triumph was drawing near. Most of us thought that the next few weeks would see a *putsch*, a forcible seizure of the reins of government. But Goering only smiled. "A *putsch* will not be necessary," he said. "We will be invited to take over. Just wait and see!" And then he rubbed his hands and caressed the jewel-studded dagger that lay on the table before him, and started speculating about the future. "The day will come," he said, "when all the world will hail our Fuehrer as the savior of humanity. Yes, you in America too," he added, nodding angrily in the direction of an American correspondent who had arched his eyebrows in quizzical skepticism. "We are on the way," went on Goering, "and nothing will stop us. I will make you a prediction: in ten years' time we Germans will be sitting on top of the world."

At those words we all smiled. Some of us, no doubt, remembered that Captain Goering had at one time been suspected of indulgence in narcotics; and some of us thought, perhaps, that he was having a little pipe dream when he spoke so boastfully. One man asked: "But Captain Goering, are you not afraid, if that is the objective of your party—I mean world conquest—that all the nations of Europe will stand together and form an alliance, and put an insuperable barrier across Germany's road in her march to world power?" And another man said, with a note of challenge in his voice: "You seem to have forgotten, Herr Goering, that it was America, in the last war, which broke the back of German aggression."

"America?" Goering laughed, and his baby-blue eyes twinkled jovially. *"Die Amerikaner, das wissen wir, sind ja die ahnungslosesten Leute in der Welt*—the Americans, we all know it, are the most unsuspecting people in the world."

Ahnungslos—unsuspecting—indeed is the argument of the isolationists!

How are we going to defend the whole Western hemisphere—which is, after all, somewhat larger than a chicken coop, with its 30,000-odd miles of coast line— if we allow the protective chain of bastions in the Atlantic Ocean which cover our hemisphere in its entirety on its Eastern side to fall into the enemy's hands? I mean, of course, the chain that runs from Greenland and Iceland to the British Isles, and from there, via the Azores and the Cape Verde Islands, to Dakar and Cape Town on the African continent.

The isolationists tell us that if it becomes necessary to defend this hemisphere—that is, if Hitler actually declares war on us and begins to move in our direction —we will make our stand at the Panama Canal and on the Caribbean islands. Time enough to worry, we are told, after Hitler has drummed up a navy big enough to offer a serious threat to that real American line of defense, the one actually existing on this continent.

But Hitler will never launch a frontal assault on Panama and the Caribbean islands, because there is a much easier way to bring the United States to its knees. He would be a fool—which he is not—to fling his head against the Panama-Caribbean bulwark, even with the aid of a captured or surrendered British navy. There is a way much more logical than the bull's tactic of assaulting the American defense line on the Atlantic seaboard. That line, it should not be overlooked, is America's only existing defense at present, and therefore would also be our last hope if the attack came in the near future. Let us not forget, either, that Hitler did not attack the Maginot Line in a head-on assault. He chose the easier way: he went around it, and took it from the rear without the loss of a single division.

What defense have we at present against a German attack on, or a German infiltration into, Brazil launched from Dakar in Africa, which is less than half the distance from New York to Brazil?

If we decide to make a stand only when Hitler, advancing from a southerly direction, attacks the Panama Canal and the Caribbean, we will no longer be defending the Western hemisphere, for in that eventuality we should already have lost the southern half of the hemisphere to the Axis. In that case we would be defending a hopelessly isolated North American continent in a desperate last-ditch stand against a German air force based in South America.

Colonel Charles A. Lindbergh has said time and again that we must be prepared to defend only the United States and the Western hemisphere. He has referred the American people to unnamed experts to find out how that is to be done. But neither he nor his experts have come forward with information on that burning subject, extremely welcome though it would be. And this for the simple reason that Colonel Lindbergh does not know—and his experts do not know, nor can they know—how to defend the whole Western hemisphere when that hemisphere's defense positions do not even exist, in the sense that they are not in our hands or under our control.

It is true we have Greenland, although no American base has yet been established near those "icy mountains" of the missionary hymn. Colonel Lindbergh has graciously approved the occupation of the subarctic island. And it must, indeed, be a valuable acquisition, if we may judge by the violent burst of temper into which the gentlemen of the Wilhelmstrasse allowed themselves to fall upon learning of the conclusion of the deal between our government and Mr. Henrik de Kauffmann, acting for the shackled Danish authorities. But Greenland is only one point in the vast stretch of this hemisphere's defenses. Greenland alone is like thunder without lightning. Without additional bases it is like the corner post of a fence without the fence. In fact, if the other links in the great potential Atlantic screen which extends in front of the American continent were to be seized by the Axis—especially if England, the mightiest naval fortress on earth, were to fall, or if Ireland were to be invaded—Greenland would quickly become a hazard to us, a stumbling block. The American position on that island would become untenable, by reason of its exposed condition. And the American garrison and matériel there would have to be Dunkirked or left to their fate.

The same applies, in turn, to Great Britain, to Dakar and to Cape Town.

If Cape Town or Dakar pass into German hands, the flank of the American Maginot Line on the Atlantic Ocean—the line Greenland-Iceland-Britain-Azores-Cape Verde-Dakar-Cape of Good Hope—has definitely been turned.

If England should fall—that is, if the keystone is knocked out of the arch—there is no longer any American Maginot Line left. Our defense simply melts into thin air. In that case, we stand alone, without the British navy, without South America, desperately clamping ourselves to what are after all mere secondary positions at Panama and in the Caribbean.

The man who peddled postcards in Vienna twenty years ago aspires to be the ruler of the world. That is unassailably true. If Hitler had no designs on the Western hemisphere, why did he not stop after the Austrian *Anschluss*, the rape of Czechoslovakia, the defeat of Poland and the debacle of France? What prevented him from merely holding on to his gains and, if England persisted in fighting on, from breaking the blockade by submarine and aërial warfare? Was he not in a perfect position to demand and obtain a complete revision of the Versailles Treaty, the aim for which he had presumably unleashed the war? Why did Berlin need the Tokyo military pact? For what purpose are the Nazis filtering into Tangier? Why are they hammering at Egypt? And why does Hitler need to capture the Mediterranean?

No, if we are on the verge of war it is not because our leadership has led us there. It is because, realistically and practically speaking, American security and independence are imminently threatened. It is because "that European war" is a world war in which distances and Maginot Lines on land or sea and even powerful navies no longer provide protection. It is because our modern civilization has developed such powerful, speedy and wide-range instruments of destruction that isolationism amounts to surrender.

Hitler's war-machine is capturing one strategic world position after the other. It is out to seize the colonial possessions of the European nations it has subdued. It is geared for a supreme dash against the Western hemisphere.

Those who mumble or shriek that invasion of America is impossible and that no foreign army will ever attempt to land on our shores, live intellectually in an age that is gone and will never return. They still think in terms of 1914 weapons, which resemble today's technically perfected war-machines as little as the phonograph compares with the radio. When the "America First" defenders speak of an impregnable defense of the Western hemisphere do they propose, in realistic language, the building and completion of an Atlantic and Pacific Maginot Line from Tierra del Fuego to Grant Land—over 30,000 miles of coast line—in time to stop Hitler's onrushing engines of destruction and conquest?

Or when, at what stage in Hitler's march around the oceans, do they consider that it will be time for us to wake up? You can fight only with pistols and knives when the burglar is on the front porch. Bombing planes and cannon in the back yard are no use then.

Armament programs are useless if you are out-maneuvered strategically before the actual fighting begins. A defense structure is futile if you are out-flanked before the first shot is fired. Czechoslovakia was unquestionably the best-prepared and best-equipped country in Europe, perhaps in the world (in proportion to her size, of course). But what did it avail her after Hitler had marched into Austria and had strategically eliminated France and Russia? Her wealth of defense matériel only helped Hitler on his march into Poland.

The defenses into which America is pouring billions of dollars will protect us only if we do not permit the Axis powers to outplay us strategically before the inevitable attack is launched. And inevitable it is!

For were we to crawl into our shell, stuff our ears against the distress signals from Britain, think ourselves into a world that ends with the North American coast line, and banish from our minds every humane sentiment—even then we could not escape the clash with Hitler's world-conquering hordes.

Hitler can be stopped only if his path to Dakar is blocked. The world-wide pincer movement of the Axis against the Western hemisphere *can* be frustrated if the African continent is not delivered to the Nazis on a silver platter. For French West Africa is, strategically, the Spain of the Battle of the Atlantic. Once under German control, it places the United States in a position as vulnerable as that of the British Empire. If Hitler is permitted to take possession of the African Atlantic coast line, the defense of the Western hemisphere becomes well-nigh impossible. He will then be poised for a leap across the ocean to the South American republics, which are by no means ready to defy him.

Keep Hitler out of Africa! should be the slogan of a genuine America First Committee. For the invasion of this hemisphere must necessarily start with the occupation of strategical bases from which aërial, naval, military and diplomatic (intrigue and propaganda) attacks can be launched in our direction. Hitler can be stopped on his march around the oceans, and his conquest of Europe can therewith be nullified, if a serious obstacle is placed in his path either at Dakar or in Egypt, in Persia or in British India. Discussing and dismissing the possibility of "an American invasion of Europe" as a hopeless and impossible gesture—as Colonel Lindbergh is doing—is talking entirely beside the point. No responsible leader in President Roosevelt's administration, nor any American military expert worthy of the

73

name, has ever suggested landing American troops in Europe.

Hitler must be prevented from marching around the oceans. He must be prevented from seizing bases in West Africa. He must be prevented from effecting a juncture with the Japanese armies in Upper India and thereafter taking the Singapore base by a joint southward march with the Japanese forces from the land side, down through Siam and the Malay Peninsula. Hitler must be prevented from encircling the American continent. An attempt to stop him by landing troops in Europe would be like closing the barn door after the horse has been stolen. Nobody has ever thought of it except Colonel Lindbergh, who uses the argument, in sheer ignorance or wittingly as demagogy, to set American public opinion on a false scent.

To prevent the encirclement of this hemisphere it is our first interest to keep our attention glued on the African continent. It is there that the land battle for the Atlantic will be fought—unless West Africa falls into Hitler's lap by reason of the fact that so far there is nobody on the spot to prevent it.

What can we do about it?

We should, without delay, either by agreement with Vichy or by force, send an expeditionary force to Dakar. Unless Pétain's government cynically acknowledges itself a military ally of Germany, it cannot and will not oppose this move. Vichy surely realizes that American occupation of Dakar would be only temporary and would, as a matter of fact, assure France's colonial rights in Africa after the war. Yet, just as Dakar fought off the landing of General de Gaulle's troops, so it might also resist an American move to occupy it. If this should happen, we must be prepared to overcome that resistance.

A similar course of action must be launched with

74

respect to the Cape Verde, Canary and Azores islands. The Portuguese and Spanish governments are no less under actual or potential Nazi control than Vichy, and it is doubtful whether they would agree peacefully to American occupation of these islands. But there can be no doubt whatsoever that the British navy, coöperating with the American fleet, can overcome any resistance that these governments could marshal.

Would this mean America's entry into the war?

It probably would, although Germany might hesitate to declare war on the United States, for fear of the reaction it would have on her own people. But even if it means supplementing our industrial war against Hitler with military action, we can no longer afford to wait. Secretary of State Hull did not exaggerate when he said that if Hitler wins, we will "stand with our backs to the wall, with the other four continents against us and the high seas lost, alone defending the last free territories on earth."

If the United States of America, which was born of the will of courageous men to live in freedom and peace, and which, under God, has become the home of a nation dedicated to the democratic-Christian ideal— if this America is worth defending, we must look the menace that confronts us straight in the face and stop dodging the real issue at stake, which is nothing less than our own national independence and freedom.

I believe the American people is a great and courageous people and that it wants to know the truth, no matter how bitter and forbidding that truth may be. For only the truth will make us free from the uncertainty, the doubts and the confusion of tongues which have of late brought us to a state resembling bedlam and to the verge of despair.

We know that the conflict raging in the world today

75

is not "that war over in Europe" but actually the limbering-up exercise of a ruthless foe for what he calls "the duel of hemispheres and continents," the preliminary for "the last great battle that must be waged in the Western hemisphere" before *"das Weltreich der Deutschen,* the world empire of the Germans" is established "for the next thousand years in history." Knowing this, we must realize in the first place that aid to Great Britain, the mighty bulwark in the enemy's path to our shores, is American self-defense, American self-help. In short, that in aiding Britain America is fighting for its own safety.

Secondly, we should draft an immediate plan of full coördination and coöperation between the American and British navies to maintain control over the world's waterways. Acting as one unit, under one command, the United States' and Britain's naval power can still stop Hitler. *Convoying of our shipments of war materials by the American fleet is, of course, essential.* Unless the decision to send convoys comes in time, and without reservations or weakening clauses, the Battle of the Atlantic will be won for Hitler, the British Isles will be reduced to ashes and our industrial war effort will be nullified.

To see America in the rôle of a mere sympathetic onlooker to Britain's tragedy is Herr Hitler's fondest desire. For his projects envisage the consecutive, separate, installment-plan conquest of Britain and America modeled on the tactics he has thus far pursued, on a miniature scale, in Europe.

It is furthermore essential that the American fleet stage a naval demonstration at Singapore. The Tokyo government must in an unmistakable manner be made to know that we are through with appeasing Japan, that we will not send another ounce of scrap or oil to support her iniquitous war against our Chinese friends, who are so valiantly standing in the breach—a breach which if it were closed would present us with a solidly hostile East Asian shore confronting our Pacific Coast. We must take the backbone out of Japanese aggression by giving Tokyo to understand that we fully appreciate the implications of the Nippon-Soviet treaty.

For by the pact concluded at Moscow in April the government of Prince Konoye has thought to obtain a diplomatic instrument with which to force America into a perpetual state of hesitation. Ostensibly, Russia has relieved Japan of preoccupations in Outer Mongolia and Manchuria, where Russia, it should be borne in mind, never threatened Japan. America is to be frightened with a Japan that can now concentrate all her attention on military and economic expansion in a southerly direction on the Asiatic continent and the Malay archipelago.

While India is still in British hands, therefore, an American force should be landed at Bombay to take up positions in the northwest provinces. This will cause Germany to halt her march to the East and will stop Japan from marching south—or, failing that, it will hurl back the Axis partners from a territory which would be the last link in the encirclement of America on the Pacific side.

If we are to stop Hitler, we must let him know now where we consider our line of defense to begin, and if he crosses that line we must be in a position to fight him.

It may mean a long war. But time will count against Hitler only if we are determined to fight him for years, if we wear him out and engage his armies at a point chosen by ourselves, while from the British Isles as a base, and from Ireland, the German industrial apparatus in Western Europe is subjected to constant and intense bombardment. In the end we will win, to be sure—but only if we start fighting now.

For then the nations in the occupied countries, too, will gain new courage, as the German people grow weary and disheartened. There will be revolts in Czechoslovakia, in Holland, in France and Norway, and the German armies will be called home to attempt to restore order—as was done in the last war—from victorious campaigns in Arabia and Turkey and the Black Sea and the Aegean.

We must proclaim our war aims: A free Germany in a free Europe in a free world! We must announce these aims over the head of the Nazi government to the now silent and inarticulate and regimented majority of the conquered peoples—and even to the German people—and rouse them to help us in lifting "the curse of Hitler" from the brows of all men.

We must promise their freedom to the peoples of India and China, set Asia ablaze from one end to the other with the ideal of democracy. The peoples must know—from a British government that will have purged itself of Toryism and Halifaxism—that the old game of imperialism and chicanery and exploitation will not start all over again if they join us in this second attempt to make and keep the world safe for democracy. The Jews, driven from pillar to post and with the ground cut off from under their feet, must have their homeland restored on both sides of the Jordan; the prisoners must be set free from the Nazi concentration camps, and everywhere the banners of the peoples must go forward.

Then the end will come for Adolf Hitler, and his dream of world conquest will vanish like mist in the rising sun of a world democracy.

It is told of the Roman Emperor Julian, who was surnamed the Apostate, that on the road to the East he stopped for a month in Antioch, the city of his youth, to rest and reëquip his legions before their arduous campaign into Persia. Donning the cloak of a philosopher one day, the Emperor strolled into the city to mingle with the crowds, to listen to the gossip in the taverns and to hear the comment of the public orators in the forum. On the way, it is said, he observed with satisfaction that his decrees against the new religion of Galilee had been strictly enforced and that the cult of Mithra had everywhere been restored to honor. Dirt and refuse lay heaped against the walls of the Christian chapels and their doors and windows had been boarded up.

Continuing his stroll, the Emperor walked into one of the populous quarters, where he espied a certain merchant by the name of Agathon, whom he had known in his youth.

Now, Agathon was one of the few in Antioch who had remained Christian.

Julian engaged the merchant in conversation, and as they stood talking together they saw the festive crowds streaming by to the marble temple of Mithra; for it was the god's anniversary, and Julian had ordered a great celebration. From afar the two men could see the white clouds of incense that rose from the altars, and to their ears came the sound of priestly music and the voices of the faithful singing hymns in praise of the sun-god.

Agathon had grown silent, but Julian suddenly laughed and asked the pensive merchant, in a bantering tone:

"Tell me, Agathon, what has become of the Carpenter of Nazareth? Is He still around?" And, pointing to the temple and the joyous multitudes, the Emperor added: "Has He any work at all these days, your Carpenter?

79

Are there still some little jobs coming His way at least?"

For a moment Agathon was still. Then, looking the Emperor in the face, he said: "Yes, Julian, the Carpenter of Nazareth is very busy these days. . . . He is nailing together a coffin for your Empire!"

Six months later Julian was no more. The Galilean had conquered.